The Shire Book

CERAMICS OF THE 1950s
Graham McLaren

1. 'Glynn Ware' vase in stoneware by Glynn Colledge for Joseph Bourne & Son (Denby), 1950s.

Printed in Great Britain by CIT Printing Services,
Press Buildings, Merlins Bridge, Haverfordwest,
Pembrokeshire SA61 1XF.

British Library Cataloguing in Publication Data:
Ceramics of the 1950s. - (The Shire book)
1. Ceramics - History - 20th century
2. Ceramic industries - Great Britain - History -
20th century I. Title 738'.0941
ISBN 0 7478 0336 6

Published in 1997 by Shire Publications Ltd,
Cromwell House, Church Street, Princes Risborough,
Buckinghamshire HP27 9AA, UK.
Copyright © 1997 by Graham McLaren. First
published 1997. ISBN 0 7478 0336 6.
Graham McLaren is hereby identified as the author of
this work in accordance with Section 77 of the
Copyright, Designs and Patents Act 1988.

COVER PHOTOGRAPH
*(Front, left to right) 'One-off' vase by Jessie Tait for Midwinter, 1957; 'bon-bon' by Hornsea,
late 1950s; 'Homemaker' pattern plate by Enid Seeney for Ridgway & Adderley, late 1950s.
(Back) Two Hornsea vases, early 1960s: (left) 'Tanglewood' and (right) 'Slip-Ware'.*

ACKNOWLEDGEMENTS
Many people have been of assistance in the production of this book. In particular I
would like to thank the following: Alexander Clement, Gordon Elliott, Jenine
Evans, Miranda Goodby, Joan McLaren, Barbara McCarthy, Kathy Niblett, Howard
Oakes, Helen Phillips, Victoria Stanton, Alan Swale, Jonathan Woodham.
Photographs are acknowledged as follows:
author's collection, 2, 4, 7, 8, 14, 15, 29, 30, 35, 37, 38, 51, 53;
City Museum and Art Gallery, Stoke-on-Trent, 1, 3, 6, 9, 17, 18, 22, 23, 27, 28,
33, 36, 39, 45, 46, 49, 50, 56, 57, 58, 59, 60, 61, 62, 64, 65, 66, 67, 70, 71;
Design Council Archive, Design History Research Centre, University of Brighton,
5, 10, 11, 12, 13, 19, 20, 21, 25, 26, 31, 40, 41, 42, 43, 44, 48, 54, 63, 69, 74;
Mrs Joan McLaren, 77; Helen Phillips, 16, 68;
the Royal Doulton Company, 24, 31, 47, 52.

CONTENTS

—CERAMICS IN THE 1950s—

The 1950s were a period of immense change for the British pottery industry. Manufacturers responded to the challenges of the post-war years by producing some of the most innovative and exciting forms and decoration seen in the twentieth century. Because of their bright colours and novel shapes, and because they evoke a feeling of the decade, ceramic objects from this period appeal to an increasingly wide public.

This explosion of new colour, decoration and design, resulting from the lifting of wartime austerity measures during the early 1950s, has been described as the 'New Look', a term first coined to describe the lavish new fashions of *hauts couturiers* such as Christian Dior. Like fashion designers, pottery manufacturers borrowed ideas from each other; and new technology made changing the surface pattern on ceramics easier, faster and cheaper than previously. As a result definite design trends emerged during the decade. These vary from the use of the imagery, if not the ideology, of the craft pottery movement to the 'surface pattern' provided by contemporary artistic movements like the American Abstract Expressionists. An emphasis on stylised patterns and motifs drawn from nature and everyday life is very noticeable, as is the use of images of travel and tourism.

Behind these design trends was the manufacturers' wish to tap into the wave of optimism and consumerism which accompanied the end of rationing. Young consumers with money to spend were to dominate the post-war era, and they wanted a more relaxed approach to dining. For this reason the New Look was felt first and most strongly in the tableware sector of the pottery industry, and in earthenware and stoneware production rather than in the 'fine china' which had always been associated with formal dining and traditional design.

Many of the established firms in the British pottery industry resisted these changes, preferring to continue marketing their products on the basis of the traditional design and fine craftsmanship which had served them so well in the past. But even these firms, faced with foreign competition and changing demands from the influential North American market, eventually saw the importance of modern design. Although a huge quantity of traditionally styled ware continued to be produced, it is with the New Look in British ceramics that this book is concerned.

A DESIGN DECADE

That the 1950s would be a period of design innovation in the British ceramic industry did not seem likely at the beginning of the decade. During the Second World War the industry had been restricted by the Utility scheme, under which many of the companies which had led the way in design during the inter-war years, such as the factory owned by the pioneering designer Susie Cooper, were either closed down or amalgamated with others for the duration of the war. Under this scheme decorated ware continued to be made, but exclusively for export and mainly for the American market in order to earn vital foreign currency for Britain. It was mostly made by firms renowned for their 'fine china', such as Royal Worcester and Josiah Wedgwood & Sons.

The emphasis was on a continuation of the decorative traditions of the industry and on the heritage of craftsmanship, which, it was hoped, would also send subtle messages to the American people about the worth of the country they were helping to defend.

The decorated ware was conservative in design and based on the tradition of floral and figurative decoration developed in the Stoke-on-Trent industry during the mid to late nineteenth century. By contrast, the Utility ware for the home market was plain and spartan. Intended mainly for people who had lost their homes through bombing and for the large number of wartime newlyweds setting up home for the first time, Utility ceramics were made of earthenware and usually based on

5

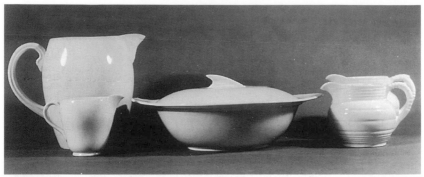

Top. 3. A range of
Utility earthenware
of the 1940s and
early 1950s by Stoke-
on-Trent manufac-
turers.

Above. 4. An image
circulated to schools
and colleges by the
Council of Industrial
Design in 1948, with
the caption: 'Now
fortunately outmoded
but still to be seen,
and avoided. The
unfunctional handle
and the decoration
provide a useful
cautionary study.'

pre-war shapes still available to
the potters.

The insistence of government on
white ware devoid of any decoration caused much tension between
industrial potters and central au-
thority during the following years.
The industry saw Utility as a di-
rect threat to the individual, eclec-
tic nature of British pottery traditions, and one of the biggest dis-
putes with the government occurred in 1943 when those con-
trolling the Utility scheme tried to
impose their own designs on the
industry.

However, it was not just because
of the necessities of war that the

government so vigorously pur-
sued the ideal of clean white func-
tional Utility pottery. Government
advisors on design policy looked
to the pre-war innovations of the
continental modernist designers,
who believed in the concept that
'form follows function', and produced designs with the minimum
of decoration. They felt that a
period of austerity could help to
banish the colourful legacy of Art
Deco and at the same time raise
the standard of public taste. To
the industry, however, this represented a profoundly alien aesthetic
ideal with left-wing, centralising
ambitions.

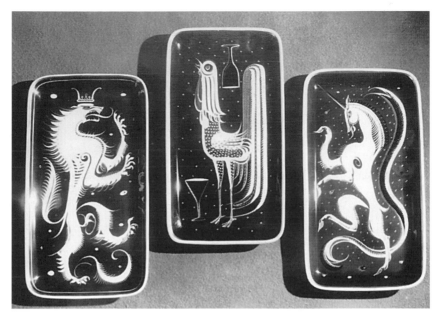

While the British public rejected the sterility of Utility design in favour of anything with colour as soon as restrictions were lifted, the scheme left a legacy of suspicion between the government and the industry well into the 1950s. Manufacturers remained concerned that the government was trying to impose alien design aesthetics on them. These were epitomised for many by the work of Pablo Picasso, who had started making ceramics at Vallauris in the south of France during 1947. The asymmetrical, sculptural quality of his work, which was exhibited in Stoke-on-Trent in 1950, and his free use of a variety of decorative methods caused a great stir. Derisively described as 'a painter's holiday', Picasso's ceramic work was a complex and subtle blend of Spanish and South American ceramic traditions with artistic impulse. Although his pieces were to influence industrial ceramics later in the 1950s, many of those who saw them for

the first time thought they represented a threat to the traditions of the British industry. With hindsight, however, we can see that they were in the vanguard of an incursion of influence on ceramic design from the fine arts, including work by Henry Moore, Barbara Hepworth, Jackson Pollock, Jean Arp and others.

The challenge presented by Picasso's work irked the industry all the more because it seemed to be officially sanctioned by the government design organisation, the Council of Industrial Design (COID). Tension between government and industry arose again in the selection of pottery for exhibition at the Festival of Britain in 1951. While the coronation of Queen Elizabeth II two years later provided the pottery industry with an opportunity to underline its traditions by producing commemorative ware which was predominantly conservative in design, the Festival organisers emphasised modernity and forward

5. Hors d'oeuvres plates in bone china by Susie Cooper exhibited in the Royal Pavilion at the Festival of Britain, 1951.

Left. 6. Plate, 'Golden Persephone' pattern by Eric Ravilious with coat of arms by Richard Guyatt for Wedgwood, 1953. Originally adapted for the coronation banquet, this design became the standard dinner ware for British embassies.

Below. 7. Plate and soup dish with crystalline pattern, 1951, designed by Peter Cave and Hazel Thumpston for the Festival Pattern Group.

thinking. Nowhere is this better shown than in the work of the Festival Pattern Group, which brought together firms manufacturing in a variety of materials, including Poole and Wedgwood in ceramics. At the centre of their work was the stylisation of crystalline and chemical patterns seen under the microscope, an early example of a fascination with the artistic possibilities of science and the 'atomic age' which was to last throughout the decade.

While hostility towards foreign design trends persisted in the early 1950s, it was also becoming clear that foreign competition was growing more intense in the most important export market of all, North America, where the market was changing rapidly and, most significantly, a new type of

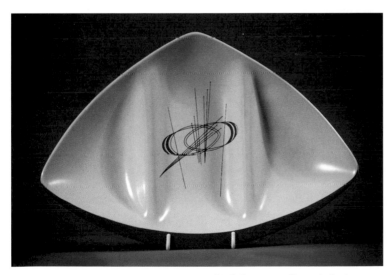

Above. 8. *Tea service with crystalline pattern by Hazel Thumpston, 1950.*

Left. 9. *Carlton Ware dish, late 1950s or early 1960s.*

consumer was emerging. This was the young adult with a high income and plenty of leisure time. The 'bridal market' (young newlyweds) in particular was ever more important, and these consumers wanted to buy tableware which was less formal and which better reflected their taste for modern styles. Increasingly they looked not to British ceramics, but to the pottery of Italy and Scandinavia.

Post-war Italian design had quickly achieved a reputation for the free, expressive use of bright

10. Square plate with 'Zebra' pattern from Italy, 1952.

colours and of abstract, sculptural form. Italian ceramics happily combined the aesthetics not just of design, but also of craft and fine art. In their freedom and expressiveness they were a complete contrast to the 'drawing board' quality of British industrial ceramics.

For those who found Italian ceramics too brash, Scandinavia offered a more comfortable interpretation of continental modernist tendencies. Whilst in Scandinavian ceramics 'form followed function' in the appropriate use of materials, they avoided the stark quality of much pre-war modernism and looked instead to crafts values and traditions for inspiration.

The consumer-led boom seen in America immediately after the war took longer to take hold in Britain, but when it came the effect on pottery design was to emphasise colour and pattern over shape. Surface pattern had always been easier to design and change than shape, and well into the 1950s many manufacturers were introducing 'contemporary' patterns on essentially pre-war shapes. This inevitably facilitated the plagiarism amongst manufacturers which occurred throughout the

11. Ornamental pottery by Richard Ginori, 1955.

decade: Lesley Jackson has made a distinction between the innovatory New Look manufacturers and the 'New Look-alikes' who copied their ideas. This emphasis on pattern was assisted by a series of technical developments, most notably the widespread introduction of photolithographic and screen printing.

Photolithography was developed during the late 1930s and was first successfully exploited commercially by American pottery manufacturers. The value of the process was that it allowed exact copies of artwork to be easily and cheaply converted into a form suitable for ceramics. These are applied to the piece using a transfer. Once the process was perfected, photolitho work was virtually indistinguishable from that done by hand, and it significantly influenced the proliferation of designs by fine artists being applied to ceramics during the 1950s. Design critics were concerned that it was able to 'cheat' the eye into thinking that it was hand decoration and that it was mainly produced for the pottery industry by independent 'litho houses', such as Johnson Matthey and Rataud, which had nothing to do with the design of shapes. They saw a danger that unscrupulous manufacturers would merely 'slap on' a variety of lithographs to inappropriate shapes.

By contrast, the introduction of the silk-screen process (first by Johnson Matthey) just after the war created a decorative approach which had an aesthetic of its own. The process favoured designs which utilised bold colours and simple, often stylised shapes. Silk-screen transfers were applied

12. 'Ceylon' coffee set designed by Hertha Bengtson and made by AB Rörstrands Porslinsfabriker, Sweden, c.1956.

13. 'Town with Boats' lithographic decoration by Castleton China, USA, 1950.

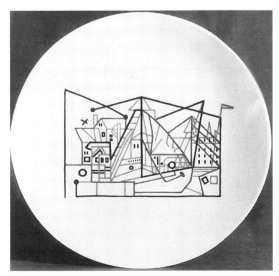

11

'on-glaze', and the decorated surface had a distinct texture which immediately revealed the method of application. The design authorities who criticised photolithography could therefore praise the 'honesty' and unique decorative effect of silk-screen.

One other process had an important impact on the decoration and also, arguably, the form of 1950s ceramics. The Murray-Curvex offset litho process was of increasing significance as it became more widely available from the middle of the decade onwards. The process involved transferring the still wet print to the piece on the bottom of a gelatine pad or 'bomb'. It allowed the printing of the internal curved sides of quite deep shapes like basins and soup bowls and made possible the all-over decoration which is so characteristic of 1950s ceramics.

14. Sugar castor and bowl in 'Riviera' pattern by Hugh Casson for Midwinter, 1954; underglaze lithographic decoration described on the backstamp as 'a genuine hand engraving'.

15. *The hugely successful 'Regatta' pattern on the 'New Elizabethan' shape, making use of on-glaze silk-screen decoration.*

16. *'Homemaker' pattern by Enid Seeney for Ridgway & Adderley, late 1950s. The 'all-over' pattern on this soup dish is an example of the decoration made possible by the Murray-Curvex process.*

17. *'Central Park' pattern on 'Gayday' shape designed by Colin Haxby, and marketed by T. G. Green in the mid to late 1950s: earthenware with on-glaze silk-screen decoration.*

THE DESIGNERS

18. Breakfast set for one in 'Quail' shape designed by Susie Cooper, 1950s; bone china with raised enamel decoration.

If there is one aspect of the 1950s which defines the decade as different from others it is the new significance given to the role of designers within the pottery industry.

The concept of the designer as a 'star' whose name alone could sell ware had its beginnings during the inter-war period with the careers of two great women designers, Clarice Cliff and Susie Cooper. Cliff, who became internationally known for her bright, Art Deco style 'Bizarre' ware during the 1920s and 1930s, took on a primarily managerial role at Newport Pottery and at A. J. Wilkinson during the post-war period, although the company continued to make prominent use of her name on backstamps for ware produced using lithographic decoration.

Susie Cooper, whose designs looked to, but did not slavishly follow, continental modernist conventions, continued to design after the war. Particularly significant was her acquisition of a bone-china business in 1950. Her designs for bone china concentrated on increasingly stylised floral motifs, developing what was described as a 'characteristically modern feathery line of pattern' and making significant use of the sgraffito decorative technique (patterns made by scratching through the unfired glaze to reveal the differently coloured body material below). Patterns like 'Spiral Fern', 'Highland Grass' and 'Whispering Grass' were exhibited throughout the decade, drawing praise for their simple, elegant modernity.

Susie Cooper's post-war work is stylistically similar to that of Eric Slater at Shelley. Slater's work concentrated on the 'sgraffito groundlay' technique, juxtaposed with

19. 'Tropic Bamboo' on 'Streamline' shape by Poole. Designed by Ann Read and marketed in 1956 exclusively through the London firm of Heal's.

20. 'Whispering Grass' pattern on 'Quail' shape in bone china; designed by Susie Cooper in 1954.

21. 'Streamline' shape by John Adams for Carter, Stabler & Adams, Poole Potteries, c.1950.

22. 'Television Set' in earthenware by A. J. Wilkinson with Clarice Cliff backstamp; late 1950s or early 1960s.

free-form swirling motifs on a bone-china body.

While some of the foundations of the New Look in 1950s ceramics were laid by such individual designers of genius, design teams, like that at Poole Pottery (Carter, Stabler & Adams), also played an

23. Two Eric Ravilious designs for Wedgwood, produced in the 1950s: (left) 'Garden'; (right) 'Persephone'.

important role. There John Adams and Truda Carter did much to promote modern pottery design before the war and continued to have an influence after it. Their designs remained in production although both had retired from the company by the early 1950s.

The larger firms tended to use in-house designers. It is a sad reflection on this sector of the industry that one of Wedgwood's best-selling design lines during the 1940s and 1950s was the pre-war work of a graphic artist and designer, Eric Ravilious, who had been killed on active service in 1942. The trade press described him as 'one of the most gifted of all in our time'. His 'Golden Persephone' pattern was adapted for the coronation of Queen Elizabeth II in 1953, and a mug originally designed for George VI's coronation in 1937 was redesigned for that of Elizabeth.

THE ROYAL COLLEGE DESIGNERS

A group of designers graduating from the Royal College of Art in London was influential in changing the role of the pottery designer. The college was established in 1837 to serve the design needs of industry but by the end of the 1930s was seen as out of date and out of touch by government and industry alike. From 1948, under Robin Darwin, the college was reorganised, acquiring a new concern for the needs of industry. In the Ceramics Department Professor Robert Baker concentrated on 'designing' designers for individual companies. As a result the department quickly developed a very positive rapport with the Stoke-on-Trent element of the industry in particular.

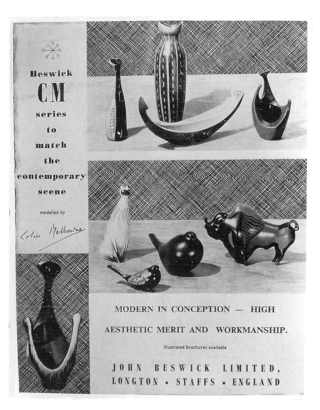

24. *Advertising copy for Colin Melbourne's 'CM' range for John Beswick Ltd, c.1956*

Perhaps the most significant of the early graduates from the department was Colin Melbourne. A ceramic sculptor by inclination, he worked both directly and as a consultant for a diverse range of companies during the 1950s, including Wade, Midwinter and Beswick. His designs excited a mixture of shock and admiration within the industry, and his work for Beswick especially, now highly collectable, shows his ability to incorporate the sculptural influence of avant-garde artists, like Henry Moore, and the ex-

17

pressive quality of Italian design to particular effect.

Similarly significant, although less wide-ranging, was Tom Arnold, who worked mainly for Ridgway & Adderley. The highly organic, sculptural shapes he produced show a clear allegiance to contemporary continental design and represent a substantial move away from British pottery traditions, whilst the more conservative 'Metro' shape (decorated with 'Conference' pattern by Pat Albeck) was given a 'Design of the Year' award by the Council of Industrial Design in 1958.

Working alongside Arnold at Ridgway was Enid Seeney, who had been apprenticed within the industry but received a one-year scholarship to the Royal College in 1954. A specialist in lithographic decoration, she made a major contribution to design of the period with her 'Homemaker' pattern, which received relatively little attention at the time but has since come to be seen as an ideal exam-

ple of contemporary 1950s ceramic design. 'Homemaker' was aimed at a young market. In its use of symbols of modern furnishing and in its wiry background (see page 13), evocative of trends in contemporary painting and the sculpture of Giacometti, it is an example of how the graphic qualities of a number of media were coming together. Working with Tom Arnold, Enid Seeney produced the pattern in bone china, as well as the original earthenware.

Whilst many of the Royal College graduates were expected to adapt to traditional design once in the industry, some companies made full use of their youthful vigour and innovative qualities. A good example is E. Brain & Company (Foley China), which employed a succession of Royal College graduates throughout the decade, including Hazel Thumpston, Peter Cave, Maureen Tanner and Donald Brindley. Thumpston had already shown her design talent while at the Royal College, work-

25. 'Park Lane' pattern by Margaret Wagg on the earthenware 'Metro' shape by Tom Arnold for Ridgway & Adderley, mid 1950s.

ing on crystalline patterns for the Festival Pattern Group. Whilst at Foley she concentrated on pattern design, such as 'Pirouette' (1955). In 1957 she collaborated with Brindley to produce 'Domino', a shape in bone china which was reported to be 'selling well in the south of England'. By 1954 Maureen Tanner had also joined Foley, quickly becoming known for lithographed bone china 'fancies', drawn in a stylised manner influenced by travelling in Italy. Tanner worked for Foley throughout the 1950s, increasingly targeting her designs at specific markets, such as Canada.

By the end of the decade graduates of the Royal College were more aware of continental trends in design, particularly those from Scandinavia, which were to dominate the 1960s. The work of Neil French and David White on the 'Royal College' shape (later renamed 'Apollo') with W. T. Copeland & Sons (Spode) heralded the new decade: its tall angular form owed more to contemporary trends on the continent and the design traditions of countries such as Sweden than to those of Britain. The shape had begun as a collaboration between college and company and was one of the final initiatives by Professor Baker before he resigned in 1959 to become design director at Worcester Royal Porcelain. 'Royal College' won the Duke of Edinburgh's Award for Elegant Design in 1960. As Spode's 'Apollo' it remained a profitable line for the company for some years.

26. 'Pirouette' pattern by Donald Brindley on 'Cresta' shape by Hazel Thumpston for E. Brain & Company (Foley China). Originally designed in 1954, this pattern was marketed exclusively through the London firm of Heal's.

27. 'Royal College' shape by Neil French and David White for W. T. Copeland & Sons (Spode), 1959.

Below. 28. 'Barbecue' pattern by Wedgwood & Company of Tunstall, 1957.

29. 'Domino' by
E. Brain &
Company (Foley
China), 1957;
shape by Donald
Brindley,
pattern by Hazel
Thumpston.

30. Bone-china
sweet dishes by
Maureen Tanner
for E. Brain &
Company (Foley
China), late
1950s: (left)
'April' for the
Cunard Steam-
ship Company;
(right) 'The Gay
Nineties'. It was
noted by the
contemporary
trade press that
these designs
were made
possible only by
the development of
photolithography.

22

THE OUTSIDERS: CONSULTANT DESIGN IN THE 1950s

David Queensberry succeeded Professor Baker at the Royal College of Art. He had already built up a strong reputation for his ability to capture a 'contemporary' feel in his designs and in 1954 had set up a consultancy with Colin Melbourne under the title of Drumlanrig Melbourne. Queensberry's work for Crown Staffordshire throughout the second half of the 1950s demonstrates this tendency but also signals a new importance accorded to the role of consultant designers, who brought in new ideas. Experiment and innovation were applauded in the consultant designer but were rarely tolerated from company designers. A design by Queensberry, 'Lines in Space' (c.1957), is an example of this; reported to have sold well in North America, it evolved from careful analysis of export market demands supplied by company representatives and by visits abroad by the designer himself.

In their handling of consultant designers, industrial manufacturers learned much from what they saw happening in America. Lucien Myers, the managing director of Poole Potteries, warned from the late 1940s of the competition that the 'California Modern' aesthetic would present to British manufacturers, and about how distinguished American designers were being employed by a newly competitive American pottery industry to provide bright, modern and attractive designs.

These tendencies were carefully noted and acted upon by Roy Midwinter of W. R. Midwinter & Company, who travelled extensively in North America during the early post-war period in order to examine and understand market tendencies. He employed as consultants a succession of well-known artists and designers, and by a frequently changing combination of bright modern photolithographic patterns and 'coupe' (or rimless) shapes he was able to keep up to date with the changing whims of consumer demand.

One of the earliest of Midwinter's consultants was Hugh Casson, whose 'Riviera' pattern (1954) proved 'supremely popular'. The hand-tinted line drawings by

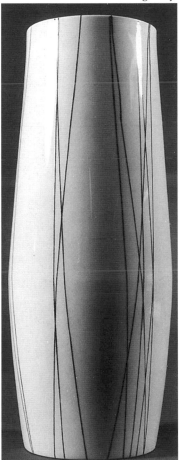

33. 'Lines in Space' (bone china) by David Queensberry for Crown Staffordshire, c.1957.

Casson were created during a holiday in the south of France. Midwinter subsequently paid him 90 guineas for the reproduction rights.

More wholeheartedly involved in the design and production process was the artist and ornithologist Peter Scott, who produced the 'Wild Geese' pattern on the 'Stylecraft' shape for Midwinter in 1955. For this pattern of flying geese, individual lithographs were specially drawn by the artist to fit each piece. The pattern was still in production in 1960, and Scott later collaborated with Beswick on a range of model china ducks.

The most significant consultant designer to work with Midwinter,

Top left. 34. Hugh Casson's 'Riviera' pattern was renamed 'Cannes' when it was adapted to fit the 'Fashion' shape by Jessie Tait.

35. Two sides of the same sugar castor decorated with 'Riviera' pattern, designed by Hugh Casson for Midwinter. They show the 'wrap-around' possibilities of lithographic decoration.

36. 'Wild Geese' pattern on 'Stylecraft' shape, designed in 1955 by Peter Scott for Midwinter.

however, was Terence Conran. Conran has dominated the British 'design industry' for over three decades but was already being advertised by Midwinter as a 'name' in the mid 1950s. Conran produced a range of patterns for the company, including 'Salad' (c.1955), 'Nature Study' (c.1956), 'Chequers' and 'Melody' (both c.1958). 'Salad' is a good example of the influences prevailing in the middle of the decade. It was advertised as being 'designed for terrace living', and in its leisurely approach to pattern, depiction of everyday objects and bold use of colour it was a clear response to contemporary design from Italy.

One of the strongest reasons for

Top. 37. 'Salad', designed by Terence Conran for Midwinter, 1955.

38. The large backstamp on 'Salad' by Terence Conran shows the heavy emphasis placed on the designer's name by the manufacturer, Midwinter.

39. 'Nature Study' by Terence Conran for Midwinter, 1955.

using consultant designers was in order to respond to design trends in other areas. The British pottery industry had a rather ambivalent relationship with the studio pottery movement, but consumers increasingly appreciated the more leisurely approach to dining (and indeed life) that ownership of hand-crafted pottery signalled. Reacting to this trend, the studio potter Kenneth Clark was employed by Joseph Bourne & Son (Denby Pottery) during the late 1950s to design both the 'Cotswold' range of ornamental ware and the 'Gourmet' series of oven-to-table ware.

This demand for new approaches to eating and living was driven by a class of young consumer with a relatively high disposable income. In North America this group was also expecting an integrated approach to interiors, and as a result British pottery manufacturers were forced to seek links in terms of

40. 'Windrush' on 'Cotswold' shape in stoneware by Kenneth Clark for Joseph Bourne & Son (Denby), 1957.

41. 'Harlequin' in earthenware by Audrey Levy for T. G. Green & Company, 1959.

Above. 42. 'Tigo Ware' by Tibor Reich for Joseph Bourne & Son (Denby), 1954: (top) 'Sisters'; (bottom left) 'Knight'; (bottom right) 'Rendezvous'.

Top right and right. 43, 44. 'Tigo Ware' by Tibor Reich for Joseph Bourne & Son (Denby), 1954.

pattern and decoration with other products such as glass, textiles and wallpaper. The British trade press launched a campaign during the late 1950s aimed at encouraging this.

Examples of such collaborations include the employment by T. G. Green & Company of Audrey Levy, a wallpaper and textile designer trained at the Royal College, who provided a series of patterns from 1959 onwards, including 'Trio', 'Harlequin' and 'Quatro'. One of the most extraordinary associations was the work for Denby of the avant-garde carpet designer Tibor Reich, who produced a huge quantity of ware ranging from the utilitarian to the sculptural, under the name of 'Tigo Ware'. His designs make strong use of contrasts between black and white and of 'peasant pottery' motifs, which underline his Hungarian origins. He turned to ceramic design owing to 'a noticeable lack of pottery which could co-ordinate with deep textured fabrics', and his work remains some of the most evocative of the decade.

For those associated with the 'traditional' element of the industry, change did not come easily. Spode, for example, introduced its 'No-Comment' barbecue plates one at a time in 1957 to test the market, while at Royal Worcester, which had been encouraged during the war to produce lavishly decorated porcelain for foreign markets, it was only at the end of the decade, with the employment of young designers like Neil French, that the contemporary trend was really acknowledged.

At Doulton the 'modern' was carefully introduced alongside the existing range of ceramics. A good example of this is the 'Desert Star' pattern introduced on the new coupe 'Avon' shape in 1955; the stylised pattern of its central motif shows the influence of the crystalline designs introduced at the Festival of Britain. Doulton's output of sculpture continued to be dominated by traditionally styled figures, although their art director, Jo Ledger, designed a small series featuring contemporary

youth (1957) intended to entice 'the younger home maker' as well as 'the more mature adult with a so-called "progressive" outlook'. Doulton also acknowledged the significance of the studio potter in their employment from 1952 of Agnete Hoy, who had previously run her own studio at Buller's, the industrial stoneware manufacturer. Her one-off and limited production pieces in salt-glaze stoneware were a modern parallel to Doulton's nineteenth-century links with art-

45. 'No Comment' barbecue plate by W. T. Copeland & Sons (Spode), 1957. The trade press noted: 'it is left to the imagination of the user as to the humorous interpretation of the design.'

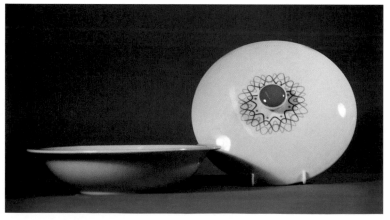

46. 'Desert Star' on 'Avon' shape by Doulton, 1955. The introduction of Murray Curvex technology allowed a pattern to be printed automatically around the knop without distortion.

Above left. 47. *Examples from the contemporary figures range depicting teenagers in various guises and introduced by Jo Ledger for Doulton in 1957. A departure from the usual type of figure production, they were known on the factory floor as 'Ledger's follies'.*

Above right. 48. *'Snowstorm' pattern in bone china by Victor Skellern for Wedgwood. Designed in 1936, it was still in production in 1957.*

ist potters like the Martin brothers.

Of all the established Staffordshire firms, however, Josiah Wedgwood & Sons probably had the most consistent attitude towards the new tendencies in design. This was largely due to the influence of the design director, Victor Skellern, who encouraged a progressive attitude in his design team as well as in the outside consultants he employed. His 'Snowstorm' pattern of 1936, for instance, predated the work of the Festival Pattern Group by some years. Skellern kept a close eye on market developments, particularly in the United States. His 'Strawberry Hill' pattern, developed in conjunction with Millicent Taplin, is an excellent example of how he managed to combine natural motifs, which pleased the tradition-

Above centre. 49. *'Strawberry Hill' pattern by Millicent Taplin, shape by Victor Skellern, Wedgwood, 1957.*

Above. 50. *(Left) 'Tennis Set' by Ridgway & Adderley, 1950s. (Right) 'Television Sandwich Set' designed by Wedgwood specifically for the 1955 Christmas season.*

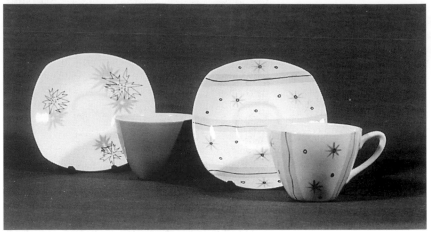

51. *Examples of the bright modern patterns and colours available on Midwinter's 'Fashion' shape, mid to late 1950s.*

52. *Advertisement for Midwinter's 'Festival' pattern on 'Fashion' shape, c.1956.*

ally oriented consumer, with a modern shape approved by the Council of Industrial Design: 'Strawberry Hill' won the 'Design of the Year' award in 1957.

The influence of the new aesthetic was most keenly felt in the competitive fields of earthenware and stoneware, and most obviously in the work of W. R. Midwinter. The Midwinter firm had already been a significant force before the war, but in the 1950s, under W. 'Roy' Midwinter, the son of the founder, it achieved dominance in the field of contemporary styling. Roy Midwinter was strongly influenced by American developments in ceramic styling, and particularly by the popularity of the rimless coupe shape. His response was to introduce first the 'Stylecraft' shape with an attenuated rim and then in 1955 a true coupe shape, 'Fashion'. These products, decorated with a variety of bright patterns, often supplied by freelance designers, were popular both at home and abroad. For the British consumer, starved of modern form and bright colour, they were 'well within the reach of the average purse' and proved a revelation. The popularity of 'Stylecraft' and 'Fashion' was boosted by a very sophisticated national marketing campaign, in women's magazines particularly. Bright, enthusiastic advertisements, which emphasised the role of ceramics in decoration and 'lifestyle', sold not just Midwinter but also the contemporary style in ceramics generally. Roy Midwinter rapidly built up a reputation in the industry for having an astute understanding of market trends; in 1957 he even launched a range of plastic tableware in partnership with Streetly Manufacturing, believing that the material was poised to present a huge challenge to the pottery industry. Marketing approaches, such as early exposure on commercial television ('Stylecraft' was featured in 1953 on the *About the Home* television programme) and boxed 'starter sets' for newlyweds, ensured that the company kept ahead of its competitors.

Although the new shapes and patterns designed by a variety of outsiders were the basis of Mid-

winter's production throughout the decade, the influence of the resident designer, Jessie Tait, was also important. Tait's work provided a coherence to Midwinter's design output throughout the decade, ranging from the avant-garde 'Festival' pattern of 1955 (described as an 'abstract portrayal of festival gaiety featuring balloons, streamers and confetti') to

53. *Midwinter's modern 'Melmex' plastic tableware, manufactured in conjunction with Streetly Manufacturing from 1957.*

54. *'Festival' pattern by Jessie Tait for Midwinter, 1955.*

55. 'One-off' vase by Jessie Tait for Midwinter, 1957. These pieces were intended to sell for less than £1 each.

56. Lamp base in earthenware by Midwinter's experimental Clayburn Studios, 1953 to 1957.

57. 'Ballet' by John Beswick, 1950s.

58. A range of 1950s vases by John Beswick.

59. John Beswick vase, mid 1950s.

the 'One-off' vase designs intended to sell for less than £1 each (1958).

The attitudes of other Staffordshire manufacturers to contemporary styles varied, but one of the best examples of a design policy which emphasised diversity and rapid change is seen at the Longton firm of John Beswick. Under the design management of Jim Hayward styles ranged from figurative decoration, which emphasised leisure activity with names like 'Dancing Days' and 'Ballet', to the wildly abstract and asymmetrical. Examples of the latter include the strangely shaped, zebra-striped vases designed by Albert Hallam and the strongly sculptural 'CM' range commissioned from Colin Melbourne (c.1956).

Other firms relied on one or two designers to provide the contemporary touch. David Queensberry's bone-china 'Queensberry' shape for Crown Staffordshire became a mainstay of its production during the mid to late 1950s and was adaptable enough to take both traditional and contemporary surface decoration. Wade adapted to the market-driven design policy by employing Colin Melbourne at their design studio (described in 1952 as 'hush-hush') to design everything from avant-garde sculptural designs to a series of small model dinosaurs in the 'Whimsies' range.

For many small and medium-sized firms in Staffordshire, 'contemporary' was just another fashion to react to, and that task usually fell to the company designer. At some firms, such as Shelley and Carlton, which had made their reputations for innovative design before the war, this process was more evolution than revolution.

Below right. 61. A pair of 1950s vases by John Beswick.

Above centre. 62. 'Mozambi' by Barker Brothers of Longton, 1950s. One of many patterns which made use of tropical flora and fauna.

Above. 63. 'Era' teapot by R. H. & S. L. Plant Ltd of Longton, 1955. The Council of Industrial Design noted: 'It has practical virtue and elegance of line, but the disc-like knob may rapidly become a 1955 cliché. The decoration is pleasant, though under vitalised.'

Shelley's reintroduction of sgraffito decoration in 1953 after an absence of thirteen years recognised its appropriateness to the prevailing fashion for the hand-crafted or 'studio' look. Carlton's designs, such as 'Windswept', from c.1958, further developed a series which gave the company's production a very distinctive image.

At J. & G. Meakin the development in 1953 of the 'Studio Ware' coupe shape provided a vehicle for a vast range of patterns targeted specifically at the North American market: the design director, Frank Trigger, spent much time in Canada surveying the market and sending back frequent reports which helped the evolution of the shape. For Palissy the hugely successful 'Regatta' pattern had

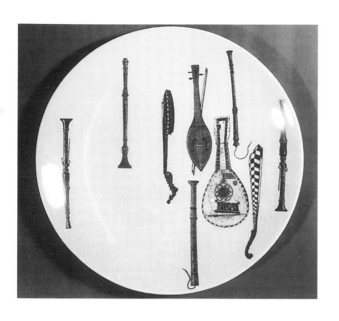

Top left. 64. *'Musicalia', with graphics by Tom Taylor, on 'Queensberry' shape in bone china for Crown Staffordshire, late 1950s.*

Top right. 65. *A small vase in the form of a cat known as 'Clara'; Wade, 1950s.*

Left. 66. *'Zamba' by Wade, c.1957. The trade advertisement suggested: 'Zamba has rhythm – the keynote of popular appeal...you can almost hear the beat of tribal drums.'*

been created through the combination of both in-house and consultant design: the 'New Elizabethan' shape to which the silk-screen transfer was applied was designed by Lady Margaret Casson. This pattern was also aimed at North America but achieved its best sales through orders from the mail-order firms such as Great Universal Stores, which expanded rapidly during the late 1950s.

THE OUT-POTTERS

By the middle of the 1950s there were about 280 industrial potteries making domestic tableware in Britain, of which around a hundred were known as 'out-potters' because they were located outside the Staffordshire manufacturing

67. Vases making use of the abstract, 'handkerchief' form and vertical line decoration which was common to many manufacturers by the late 1950s. Arthur Wood & Son, 1957.

Below. 68. 'Habitant' pattern on 'Studio Ware' shape by J. & G. Meakin, c.1953.

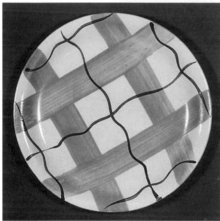

Above. 69. 'Ripple' by A. B. Read for Poole, 1955.

Left. 70. Oil jar (left) and shaker (right) in earthenware designed by John Clappison for Hornsea, late 1950s.

district. Many of these companies were among the most innovative in terms of design and they were at the forefront of the movement towards more modern design.

Some of these companies had already established their credentials for innovation before the war. The firm of Carter, Stabler & Adams, known as 'Poole' after 1952, relied during most of the period on an updated version of its famous coupe 'Streamline' shape introduced just before the war, and it was not until 1958, with

71. Poole ware from the 1950s: (left) flower troughs designed by A. B. Read, c.1955; (right) teapot in 'Contour' shape by Robert Jefferson, 1959, in mottled semi-grey glaze.

72. A range of earthenware manufactured by Hornsea between the mid 1950s and the early 1960s.

73. So-called 'Slip-Ware' earthenware flower vase and bowl, Hornsea, early 1960s.

the employment of Robert Jefferson, that the first true post-war shape, 'Contour', was introduced.

While Poole is an example of an innovatory pottery in the south of England, a parallel can be found in the north-east at Hornsea, East Yorkshire, where in 1949, on the site of an old brickworks, Desmond and Colin Rawson established a company producing 'fancies'. They quickly became known for their innovative approach, employing designers such as John

Clappison to produce shapes which, in their asymmetry and emphasis on surface texture and colour, looked startlingly modern. They rapidly gained official sanction and approval by inclusion on Council of Industrial Design lists during the late 1950s. Hornsea's production during this period was very diverse, ranging from vase forms, which are highly reminiscent of the most advanced work in studio ceramics (the work of Lucie Rie and Hans Coper seems to have been particularly influential), to rather twee earthenware 'fancies' aimed at the souvenir trade.

Other out-potters targeted very specific sectors of the market. An example is the firm of Denby, located near Derby, which became known for its oven-to-table ware, a relatively new field during this period. Denby recognised the possibilities of a link with the aesthetics of craft pottery, and consequently much of their production has an almost handmade look to it, with a colour range emphasising homely greens and browns. In this they were assisted by Glynn Colledge, who was essentially a studio potter working within a factory environment. Colledge produced both designs for mass production and 'Glynn Ware', a more limited range mainly composed of hand-decorated vessel forms. A particularly good example of Denby's astute combination of craft aesthetics with business acumen was the success of the 'Greenwheat' pattern (c.1956), which was fully released on to the market only after exhaustive customer surveys, which tested its popularity against ten other possible patterns.

Denby competed in the oven-

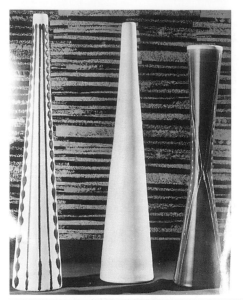

Top. 74. 'Cheviot' vases by Glynn Colledge for Joseph Bourne & Son (Denby), 1956.

Above. 75. Updated range of 'Cornish Kitchen Ware' by Berit Ternell for T. G. Green & Company, 1959.

to-table ware market with the firm of T. G. Green & Company of Church Gresley, Derbyshire. This firm had become well-known for its blue and white banded 'Cornish Cookware' range, which was one of the very few examples of British ceramic design the historian and critic Nikolaus Pevsner

76. Coffee set in porcelain by William E. Gordon at the Walton Pottery, Chesterfield, 1954.

found it possible to admire when he considered the design standards of the industry in 1937. During the late 1950s the company launched a new design initiative which brought it to the attention of the Council of Industrial Design. It employed the Swedish designer Berit Ternell to update the range to include oven-to-table ware, which was much praised for its simple elegance. The company launched a major advertising campaign on the basis of its designs and designers, for instance Audrey Levy's 'Trio' pattern and Colin Haxby's 'Central Park' silk-screen design for the 'Gayday' shape. However, although it was claimed that these new patterns were innovative, many were simply bought from the stock of the litho houses. The fact that 'Central Park' was being discussed as a Johnson Matthey silk-screen pattern as early as 1954 serves to emphasise the importance of these organisations to the development of surface pattern on ceramics during the early 1950s.

Alongside these relatively large firms, the work of smaller potteries

must not be overlooked. Typical of these was Sandygate, a firm at Newton Abbot, Devon, which, it was noted in 1958, 'occupies a position somewhere midway between the studio and the industrial potter, enjoying most of the advantages of the latter, together with many of the capabilities of the former, especially that of being able to align itself very quickly to fashion changes'. This meant that the firm produced anything that seemed to be currently successful, from polkadot tableware (early 1950s) to vases in the black and white sgraffito style (c.1957).

By the end of the 1950s pottery manufacturers were facing difficult economic conditions at home and increasing competition abroad. Over the next decade there was a general move towards the amalgamation of firms into the large 'groups' which characterise the pottery industry today. The idiosyncrasy and exuberance which marked so much pottery design of the 1950s was largely quelled, although the 'look' continued in the work of firms such as Hornsea. Perhaps the most powerful legacy of the decade was the significance accorded to the designer. At Portmeirion, for instance, Susan Williams-Ellis has produced a series of highly successful designs, continuing the tradition of female involvement in this aspect of the pottery business. One of the earliest, 'Malachite' of 1959, was produced simultaneously in pottery, Axminster carpet and furnishing fabric, so acknowledging the revolution in consumer demand which had brought such far-reaching changes to the pottery industry during the 1950s.

FURTHER READING

Batkin, M. *Wedgwood Ceramics 1846-1959: A New Appraisal.* Richard Dennis, 1982.
Baynton, V.; May, H.; and Morton, J. *The Beswick Collector's Handbook.* Kevin Francis, 1986.
Buckley, C. *Potters and Paintresses – Women Designers in the Pottery Industry 1870-1955.* The Women's Press, 1990.
Dex, L. *Hornsea Pottery – A Collector's Guide, 1947-1967.* Beck Books, 1989.
Eatwell, A. *Susie Cooper Productions.* Victoria and Albert Museum, 1987.
Hannah, F. *Ceramics – Twentieth Century Design.* Bell & Hyman, 1986.
Hawkins, J. *The Poole Potteries.* Barrie & Jenkins, 1980.
Jackson, L. *The New Look – Design in the Fifties.* Thames & Hudson, 1991.
Niblett, K. *Dynamic Design – The British Pottery Industry 1940-1990.* Stoke-on-Trent City Museum and Art Gallery, 1990.
Opie, J. *Scandinavia – Ceramics and Glass in the Twentieth Century.* Victoria and Albert Museum, 1989.
Peat, Alan. *Midwinter – A Collector's Guide.* Cameron & Hollis, 1992.
Walker, S. *Queensberry Hunt – Creativity and Industry.* Fourth Estate, 1992.
Watkins, C.; Harvey, W.; and Senft, R. *Shelley Potteries.* Barrie & Jenkins, 1986.
Watson, O. *British Studio Pottery.* Phaidon, 1990.
Woodhouse, A. *Susie Cooper.* Trilby, 1992.

PLACES TO VISIT

Before travelling, intending visitors are advised to telephone to find out the opening times and to establish that relevant items will be on display.

Bristol City Museum and Art Gallery, Queen's Road, Bristol BS8 1RL. Telephone: 0117-922 3571.
British Museum, Great Russell Street, London WC1B 3DG. Telephone: 0171-636 1555.
The Design Museum, Butler's Wharf, Shad Thames, London SE1 2YD. Telephone: 0171-403 6933.
Manchester City Art Galleries, Mosley Street, Manchester M2 3JL. Telephone: 0161-236 5244.
Royal Museum of Scotland, Chambers Street, Edinburgh EH1 1JF. Telephone: 0131-225 7534.
The Royal Pavilion, Pavilion Buildings, Brighton, East Sussex BN1 1EE. Telephone: 01273 603005.
Stoke-on-Trent City Museum and Art Gallery, Bethesda Street, Hanley, Stoke-on-Trent, Staffordshire ST1 3DE. Telephone: 01782 202173.
The Victoria and Albert Museum, Cromwell Road, South Kensington, London SW7 2RL. Telephone: 0171-938 8500.

77. 'Greenwheat' pattern by Joseph Bourne & Son (Denby), c.1956.